SCARY PLACES

Dark Mansions

Credits

Cover and Title Page, © Konradbak/Fotolia and Peter D./Shutterstock; 4–5, © Lukasz Pajor/Shutterstock; 6, © Marius Jaecklin; 7T, © The NYPL Digital Picture Collection; 7C, © The Granger Collection, New York; 7B, © Boone Callaway; 8, © Barbara Q. Bennet; 9, © Photoservice Electa/SuperStock; 10, © Steven Bosworth/snbphoto.co.uk; 11T, © Press Association via AP Images; 11B, © Michelle Enfield/Alamy; 12, © Craig S. Majors; 13, © StudioSmart/Shutterstock; 14, © AP Photo/Morry Gash; 15T, © Bettmann/Corbis; 15C, © Wisconsin Historical Society (WHi-3970); 15B, © Hemis.fr/SuperStock; 16, © Frank Dimas Aguero; 17, Art by Kim Jones; 18, © Marc Leonard; 19T, © K. Jacob Ruppert, J.D., New York/New Orleans; 19B, © thieury/Shutterstock; 20, © Rachel Fagen; 21, Art by Kim Jones; 22, © Dean C. Garrett Jr.; 23T, © Mervyn Rees/Alamy; 23B, © Joslyn Smith; 24, © Dennis Mott; 25, © NaturePL/SuperStock; 26, © Robert Johnson; 27, © Museum of the City of New York/The Granger Collection, New York; 31, © Asier Villafranca/Shutterstock; 32, © Henrik Larsson/Shutterstock.

Publisher: Kenn Goin
Editorial Director: Adam Siegel
Creative Director: Spencer Brinker
Design: Dawn Beard Creative
Cover Design: Dawn Beard Creative and Kim Jones
Photo Researcher: Picture Perfect Professionals, LLC

Library of Congress Cataloging-in-Publication Data

Williams, Dinah.
  Dark mansions / by Dinah Williams.
    p. cm. — (Scary places)
  Includes bibliographical references (p.) and index.
  ISBN 978-1-61772-457-2 (library binding) — ISBN 1-61772-457-2 (library binding)
  1. Haunted houses. I. Title.
  BF1475.W54 2012
  133.1'22—dc23
                          2011044908

For more information, write to Bearport Publishing Company, Inc., 45 West 21st Street, Suite 3B, New York, New York 10010. Printed in the United States of America in North Mankato, Minnesota.

10 9 8 7 6 5 4 3 2 1

Contents

Dark Mansions

A big, beautiful **mansion** sounds like a great place to live. Yet what if sad **spirits** haunt the hallways and ghostly screams echo out of the large windows? No amount of money can stop a house like that from becoming a horror.

What turns a grand and beautiful home into a haunted one? Perhaps the reason is that its many rooms hold memories of only pain and suffering. Among the 11 haunted mansions in this book, you'll discover a beautiful **plantation** where a ghostly hound howls on stormy nights; Manhattan's oldest home, where a spirit shushes schoolchildren; and an **architect**'s dream house, which turned into a nightmare with the swing of an ax.

Old House, Old Ghost

The Morris-Jumel Mansion, New York, New York

Many famous people visited the New York mansion that was built in 1765 by British colonel Roger Morris and became known as Mount Morris. In 1776, George Washington used it as his headquarters while he was fighting the British during the Revolutionary War (1775–1783). In 1790, Washington dined there with future presidents John Adams and Thomas Jefferson. Of course, none of these famous visitors stayed nearly as long as homeowner Eliza Jumel.

The Morris-Jumel Mansion is the oldest surviving house in Manhattan.

Wealthy French wine merchant Stephen Jumel bought Mount Morris—which would become known as the Morris-Jumel Mansion—with his wife, Eliza, in 1810. In 1832, Jumel fell from a carriage and was seriously injured. He died shortly after, leaving Eliza his vast fortune. Not everyone believed the accident had killed him, though. People whispered that Eliza had loosened the bandages that covered his wounds, causing him to bleed to death.

Eliza Jumel

The **rumors** didn't stop when Eliza married former vice president Aaron Burr a short time later. After Burr's death in 1836, Eliza lived alone in the mansion and started acting strangely. Some said she went mad. She died in 1865 at age 90. Since the house became a museum in 1904, people have claimed to see her ghost wandering the halls. Reportedly, she wears a purple dress and knocks loudly on doors and windows.

Aaron Burr was vice president of the United States from 1801 to 1805.

In 1964, schoolchildren were visiting the mansion. While they were playing and making noise on the lawn, a woman came out on the balcony and told them to be quiet. The woman was later identified, based on the clothing she was wearing, as the ghost of Eliza Jumel.

Inside the Morris-Jumel Mansion

"Come Play with Me"

Kehoe House, Savannah, Georgia

Tourists in Savannah's historic district expect to see cobblestone streets, beautiful mansions, and moss-covered oak trees. What they don't expect is to hear otherworldly voices calling, "Play . . . come play with me." Could these voices coming from the Kehoe House be those of ghostly children looking for a playmate?

The Kehoe House

In 1892, wealthy businessman William Kehoe built a mansion large enough for his ten children. The five-story redbrick building, which still stands today, has more than a dozen bedrooms. There are brass and marble chandeliers, a courtyard garden, and 18 fireplaces. According to **legend**, two of the Kehoe children met their end in one of these fireplaces. The twin boys are said to have died in an accident while playing in the chimney. After their deaths, the fireplace **mantel** was decorated with angels in their memory.

William Kehoe died in 1929, and the house was sold a year later. Since then, it has become a **luxurious inn**—with some ghostly guests! Visitors have heard children running and playing in the halls at night. Yet no children were ever staying at the inn at the time. One night, a guest in room 201 awoke to a small hand on her cheek. She opened her eyes to the sight of a young boy, who quickly disappeared. Was he playing a ghost's version of hide-and-seek?

William Kehoe's favorite spot in the house was the **cupola**. A light has been seen burning there late into the night. However, staff members at the inn say they don't go up there. As a result, people say that William is still working upstairs—in the form of a ghost.

Chased from Their Mansion

Clifton Hall, Nottingham, England

More than 700 years ago, Clifton Hall started out as a fairly small stone house with a built-in **watchtower**. However, its owners expanded the building over the centuries to include 52 rooms. Among them are 17 bedrooms, a gym, a movie theater, and 10 bathrooms. So why does this huge and historic mansion stand empty? According to its recent owners, there is a simple answer—ghosts.

Clifton Hall

Millionaire Anwar Rashid moved into Clifton Hall with his family in 2007. During their first night there, family members heard someone pounding on the walls. Then an unknown man's voice said, "Is anyone there?" After a long search, the Rashids couldn't find anyone in the house. A few months later, Anwar's wife saw what looked like her daughter downstairs at 5:00 A.M. Yet when she checked the girl's room, she was asleep in her bed.

Anwar Rashid

For eight months, the family was **pestered** by spirits— or at least by unexplained sights and sounds. Finally, when Mr. and Mrs. Rashid found drops of blood on their baby's quilt, the strange happenings became too much for them. They fled the house and have never returned. After the horrible **ordeal**, Anwar Rashid said, "The ghosts didn't want us there, and we could not fight them because we couldn't see them."

During their stay, the family called **paranormal investigators**, but these experts could not drive the spirits from the house. In fact, two investigators fainted after seeing the ghost of a boy.

Underground Railroad Horror

Hannah House, Indianapolis, Indiana

People who visit the Hannah House sometimes find that it smells of death and decay. For years, no one has understood why. Perhaps it is because those who died there were hidden in the basement—and their presence can still be felt.

The Hannah House

Before the **Civil War** (1861–1865), slaves sometimes tried to escape to places in the North where slavery was illegal. They often traveled at night. During the day, they'd hide at houses owned by people who were **opposed** to slavery. The Hannah House was one such station in what was called the **Underground Railroad**. The owner of this stately brick mansion, Alexander Hannah, hid slaves in his basement.

One day, according to stories people in Indianapolis have told, a group of slaves were crowded in the Hannah House basement. An oil lamp was accidentally knocked over. The fire spread quickly. Everyone hiding died in the flames. Hannah couldn't let people know he had been secretly helping slaves, so he buried their bodies in the basement.

In 1899, the mansion was sold to the Oehler family. Since then, the house has shown many signs of being haunted. Doors have opened and closed on their own. A chandelier has rocked without any wind present, and paintings have fallen from the walls. Most disturbingly of all, people have heard moans and seen ghosts in the shadows of the basement.

The Hannah House is not the only haunted mansion in Indianapolis. A few miles north of it is the James Allison Mansion. Now owned by Marian University, it features a one-ton (907-kg) silver chandelier and a Tiffany stained-glass ceiling. The house also has a pool in the basement, where a baby once drowned. According to some, the young child's crying is still heard today.

Ax Murder at an Architect's Home

Taliesin, Spring Green, Wisconsin

Famed architect Frank Lloyd Wright fell in love with a woman named Mamah Borthwick in 1909. He built her a beautiful home, where he hoped they would grow old together. Instead, it became the site of her murder.

Taliesin

Taliesin, which means "shining brow" in Welsh, is the name Frank Lloyd Wright gave to the mansion he built for Mamah Borthwick. The name is fitting, since the long building was perched on a "brow" of a hill overlooking the Wisconsin River. In 1911, Wright moved in with Mamah and her two children.

Frank Lloyd Wright

On August 15, 1914, Wright had to travel to Chicago on business. When Mamah, her children, and some workers went inside the house for lunch, the Wright family's butler, Julian Carlton, was waiting. He locked the dining room doors and set fire to the room. Carlton used an ax to attack anyone who tried to escape the flames. He killed seven people, including Mamah Borthwick and her children. Their bodies were taken by firefighters to a cottage on the property.

Mamah Borthwick

Mamah was buried on the grounds of Taliesin. Over the next few years, Wright rebuilt the mansion "to wipe the scar from the hill." Since that time, Borthwick's spirit has been seen by visitors. She is said to wander near the cottage where her body was taken after the fire.

Taliesin was destroyed again by an electrical fire in 1925. It was rebuilt a final time and served as Wright's studio. Here, he designed his most famous buildings—the Guggenheim Museum in New York and Fallingwater in Pennsylvania.

The Guggenheim Museum

A Horrible Hostess

Lalaurie House, New Orleans, Louisiana

No one passed up an invitation to Madame Lalaurie's house. She was a rich, important person in New Orleans during the early 1800s, and she threw fancy parties where people danced and dined. However, while the music played and guests enjoyed themselves, they had no idea of the horrors their hostess hid from them in the attic above.

Lalaurie House

Dr. Louis Lalaurie and his wife, Delphine, moved into their beautiful three-story mansion in 1832. Dozens of slaves spent all day keeping it clean. Yet Madame Lalaurie was never satisfied. To make the slaves work harder, she would beat them—and worse.

In 1834, a fire broke out in the house. Rescuers raced through the rooms. When they reached the attic, they crashed through the locked door. There they found startling evidence of Madame Lalaurie's cruelty. Slaves were chained to the walls. They had been beaten and were weak with hunger. One man had open wounds all over his body.

When newspapers reported the horrible **abuse**, the people of New Orleans were shocked and wanted Madame Lalaurie to pay for her crime. When they couldn't find her, a **mob** descended on the mansion, nearly destroying the inside of the house.

As the years passed, the building became a school, a bar, and finally, an apartment house. Despite the changes, however, the ghostly screams of the victims of Madame Lalaurie's cruelty were still heard within its walls. Today, the Lalaurie mansion is said to be one of the most haunted places in New Orleans.

What happened to Madame Lalaurie? She escaped by carriage when the mob attacked her house. Some say the family fled to Paris. She was never arrested for hurting so many people. Perhaps that is why the ghosts of her victims still haunt her home.

Madame Lalaurie

Mob Murder in a Haunted Mansion

Kreischer Mansion, Staten Island, New York

For many years, Charles Kreischer's mansion on Arthur Kill Road was thought to be haunted. Perhaps that is because of his family's tragic history. While their story is heartbreaking, it is not as terrible as what happened in the house a century later.

The Kreischer Mansion

Balthasar Kreischer moved his family from Germany to America in 1836. A year earlier, many of New York City's wooden buildings had been destroyed by a giant fire. As a result, Kreischer was able to make a fortune manufacturing fireproof brick from Staten Island clay. Around 1885, he built matching mansions on a hill for his sons, Charles and Edward, who worked with him in the business.

Balthasar Kreischer

During the 1890s, the series of terrible events that would lead to the talk of ghosts began. First the Kreischer brick factory burned down. Then, with the business failing and much of the family fortune lost, Edward shot himself in the head. Finally, in 1930, Edward's house burned down, leaving the Charles Kreischer house the only mansion on the hill.

Many years later, in 2005, a man named Joseph Young was hired by the mansion's new owners to take care of the house while it was empty. Shockingly, Young's other job was as an **assassin** for an **organized crime** group—in other words, the Mob. A New York Mob boss hired Young to kill a man named Robert McKelvey. Young brought him to the Kreischer mansion and carried out the murder there—drowning his victim in a pond that had been decorated with Kreischer bricks.

One ghost that has been said to haunt the Kreischer Mansion is Edward's wife, who can be heard crying over his death. Another is a cook who once worked for the Kreischers— and who is now heard clanging pots and pans.

Salem's Sheriff

Joshua Ward House, Salem, Massachusetts

In 1692, more than 150 people in Salem were arrested on **suspicion** of witchcraft. Many of those **accused** were tortured until they **confessed**. Sheriff George Corwin got more than a confession from Giles Corey. He got a **curse** as well. Some say that curse may have left the sheriff unable to find rest—and driven him to haunt a Salem mansion.

Joshua Ward House

George Corwin was the high sheriff of Essex County. During the witch trials, he often forced confessions. One way he did that was to pile stones on the chest of the accused until he or she pleaded guilty. Giles Corey, an 80-year-old farmer, was one of those who refused to lie and say he practiced witchcraft. As a result, he was crushed to death by the weight of the stones. Some say he died cursing the cruel sheriff.

After causing numerous deaths, Corwin died a hated man in 1696. So that no one could damage his body in revenge, he was originally buried in the basement of his home. Later, in the 1780s, Joshua Ward, a wealthy sea captain, built his mansion where Corwin's house had once stood. Within it, Corwin's ghost has reportedly been causing trouble ever since. Candles have mysteriously been melted and bent into the shape of an "S." When the building was an inn during the late 1800s, guests reported seeing a man's ghost sitting by the fireplace. Later, when it was a business, the security alarm went off 60 times in two years without explanation.

Giles Corey being crushed to death

In the 1980s, the mansion was used as a real estate office. One day, pictures of the employees were taken. When one was printed, instead of the employee, it showed a frizzy-haired woman with a long gray coat. Some believe it is the ghost of one of the accused witches sent to her death by George Corwin.

21

California's Most Haunted

Whaley House, San Diego, California

The Whaley House has stood on San Diego Avenue for more than 150 years. From the moment it was built where the city's old **gallows** had once stood, it has reportedly been home to ghosts. In fact, so many visitors have seen spirits there, it is considered by some to be the most haunted house in California.

The Whaley House

In 1852, a man called Yankee Jim Robinson was sentenced to die for stealing a boat. Store owner Thomas Whaley was one of many present to see him hang. Four years later, Whaley built his two-story brick mansion right on the empty lot where the gallows had once stood. Soon after his family moved in, heavy footsteps were heard in the house. Remembering what had happened at the site, Whaley became convinced that it was the ghost of Yankee Jim.

A gallows

In 1960, Thomas Whaley's house became a museum. Since that time, not only Yankee Jim but also several other spirits from the Whaley family's days have appeared. Thomas's ghost has been spotted at the top of the stairs, while the ghost of his wife, Anna, has been seen both downstairs and in the garden. A long-haired girl is said to dart through the dining room. Legend has it that she was playing with the Whaley children in the backyard and broke her neck when she ran straight into the clothesline. Even the ghost of the Whaleys' dog has been seen running down the hall of the mansion.

Like Thomas Whaley, Yankee Jim is said to haunt the mansion's stairs. If what people say is true, that is because the stairs are in the exact spot where the gallows once stood. Some visitors have also said that they have felt a **noose** tightening around their necks as they passed through the house.

The staircase inside the Whaley House

23

A Tale of Two Ghosts

Rotherwood House, Kingsport, Tennessee

In 1818, Reverend Frederick Ross built Rotherwood on a plantation located along the Holston River. The gorgeous, three-story mansion had plenty of room for his large family. Over the years, it would also become home to two very different ghosts—one a kind and beautiful woman, and the other a cruel and much-hated man.

Rotherwood House

Reverend Ross had eight sons and a daughter named Rowena. Lovely and well educated, she became engaged to a man from a neighboring town. One day he went fishing on the Holston River. As Rowena watched in horror from the shore, her fiancé's boat **capsized** and he drowned.

After two years, Rowena married another man. However, before long, he died of yellow fever. She later remarried and had a daughter, but her daughter died at a young age. Deeply saddened by so many losses, Rowena took her own life—according to many accounts, she drowned herself in the river where her first love had died. Ever since, people have seen her ghost at night pacing its banks.

Joshua Phipps, a greedy and brutal slaveholder, became the second owner of Rotherwood—and the second ghost said to haunt it. After years of beating and cruelly overworking the plantation's slaves, Phipps became ill. According to legend, a black cloud of flies descended on his sickbed. They filled his mouth and nose, suffocating him. Some say that his horrible death was the result of a curse placed on him by those he had abused. Phipps's spirit is said to still haunt Rotherwood. Unlike Rowena, Joshua Phipps is a noisy ghost who likes to laugh and scream.

People say that at Joshua Phipps's funeral in 1861, the sky went dark and his coffin began to shake. Out of the coffin leaped a huge black dog. Known as the "Hound from Hell," the dog is still heard howling on stormy nights.

A Deadly Mansion

The Lemp Mansion, Saint Louis, Missouri

People say, "Money can't buy happiness." This idea is especially true for the Lemps, a rich family plagued by tragedy. Their misery was so great that it did not end with death. According to some, the Lemp Mansion is still home to their sad souls.

The Lemp Mansion

In the late 1800s, William Lemp's family made huge amounts of money brewing beer. The vast fortune enabled Lemp to turn his 33-room mansion into a showplace. The home had its own elevator, a glass room filled with exotic birds, and three **vaults** just to house the family's treasures.

The family's luck changed, however, when Lemp's son Frederick died of heart failure in 1901. Devastated, William shot himself in the head three years later. Another son, William Jr., then took over the business. When drinking beer became illegal during **Prohibition**, he shut down the brewery and sold it in the 1920s. The Lemp family never recovered. Over the next 30 years, three more Lemps shot themselves: William Jr.; his sister, Elsa; and his brother Charles.

New owners turned the mansion into an inn in 1975. That was when visitors began noticing the ghosts. Locks opened and closed, lights turned on and off, voices came from empty rooms, and a piano played by itself. Guests in William Sr.'s room heard ghostly footsteps run up the stairs and kick the door. Supposedly, William Jr. had done this when he'd heard the gunshot that killed his father.

Below the Lemp Mansion is a natural **cavern**, where beer was once stored because of the naturally cool temperatures there. The Lemp family also had a ballroom, an auditorium, and a swimming pool built into the cave. Today, these underground areas are abandoned.

The Lemp Brewing Company

Taliesin
Spring Green, Wisconsin

Frank Lloyd Wright's famous home is also the site of an infamous murder.

Hannah House
Indianapolis, Indiana

Spirits linger in this station on the Underground Railroad.

Whaley House
San Diego, California

For more than 150 years, ghosts have roamed this site of a former gallows.

The Lemp Mansion
Saint Louis, Missouri

This grand home is the setting for a rich family's tragic events.

Joshua Ward House
Salem, Massachusetts

The Salem witch trials are still having an effect on a sea captain's former home.

The Morris-Jumel Mansion
New York, New York

The oldest home in Manhattan is inhabited by a cranky ghost.

Kreischer Mansion
Staten Island, New York

Fires and a Mob-related murder make this mansion horrifying.

Kehoe House
Savannah, Georgia

The playful ghosts of twin boys visit guests at this historic inn.

Lalaurie House
New Orleans, Louisiana

A wicked slaveholder's crimes still haunt this New Orleans mansion.

Rotherwood House
Kingsport, Tennessee

A heartbroken ghost and an evil hound both haunt this house on a river.

NORTH

AMERICA

Pacific Ocean

SOUTH

AMERICA

Atlantic Ocean

Arctic
Ocean

EUROPE

ASIA

Clifton Hall
Nottingham, England

A 13th-century mansion is plagued by meddlesome spirits.

AFRICA

Indian
Ocean

AUSTRALIA

N
W E
S

Southern
Ocean

ANTARCTICA

Glossary

abuse (uh-BYOOSS) harmful treatment

accused (uh-KYOOZD) blamed for or charged with a crime or doing something wrong

architect (AR-ki-tekt) a person who designs buildings and makes sure they are built properly

assassin (uh-SASS-in) a person who carries out a carefully planned murder

capsized (KAP-syezd) turned over in the water

cavern (KAV-urn) another word for *cave*

Civil War (SIV-il WOR) the U.S. war between the Southern states and the Northern states, which lasted from 1861 to 1865

confessed (kuhn-FEST) admitted that one has done something wrong

cupola (KYOO-puh-luh) a round structure built on top of a roof

curse (KURSS) words spoken to cause evil or injury; a spell

gallows (GAL-ohz) a wooden structure from which criminals are hanged

inn (IN) a small hotel

legend (LEJ-uhnd) a story handed down from the past that may be based on fact but is not always completely true

luxurious (lug-ZHUR-ee-uhss) very comfortable and of high quality

mansion (MAN-shuhn) a very large and grand house

mantel (MAN-tuhl) a covering, which is often decorated, for a fireplace

mob (MOB) a large group of angry people

noose (NOOS) a large loop at the end of a piece of rope

opposed (uh-POHZD) to be against something

ordeal (or-DEEL) a difficult experience

organized crime (OR-guh-*nyezd* CRYEM) groups that plan and carry out different kinds of illegal activities, such as robbery, gambling, and smuggling

paranormal investigators (*pa*-ruh-NOR-muhl in-VEST-uh-*gay*-torz) people who study events or collect information about things that cannot be scientifically explained

pestered (PEST-urd) bothered or annoyed

plantation (plan-TAY-shuhn) a large farm where crops such as cotton or tea are grown

Prohibition (*proh*-uh-BISH-uhn) a period in American history, lasting from 1920 to 1933, during which the sale of alcoholic beverages was against the law

rumors (ROO-murz) stories that are told by many people but are not necessarily true

spirits (SPIHR-its) supernatural creatures, such as ghosts

suspicion (suh-SPISH-uhn) belief of guilt for a crime

Underground Railroad (UHN-dur-*ground* RAYL-rohd) a series of safe places in which slaves could stay while trying to escape to freedom in the years before the U.S. Civil War

vaults (VAWLTS) rooms for keeping valuables safe

watchtower (WOCH-*tou*-ur) a tall structure from which people can look out for enemies or other dangers

Bibliography

Austin, Joanne. *Weird Hauntings: True Tales of Ghostly Places*. New York: Sterling (2006).

Brown, Alan. *Stories from the Haunted South*. Jackson, MS: University Press of Mississippi (2004).

Holzer, Hans. *Ghosts: True Encounters with the World Beyond*. New York: Black Dog & Leventhal (2005).

Read More

Krohn, Katherine. *Haunted Houses*. Mankato, MN: Edge Books (2006).

Oxlade, Chris. *The Mystery of Haunted Houses*. Chicago: Heinemann Library (2006).

Parvis, Sarah. *Haunted Hotels (Scary Places)*. New York: Bearport (2008).

Williams, Dinah. *Haunted Houses (Scary Places)*. New York: Bearport (2008).

Learn More Online

To learn more about dark mansions, visit
www.bearportpublishing.com/ScaryPlaces

Index

About the Author

Dinah Williams is a nonfiction editor and writer who has produced dozens of books for children. She lives in New Jersey.